SIMON DE LA PEÑA

Isaiah Six Worship

Contents

1

Chapter 1

Psalm 22:4 (TLV)

4 Yet You are holy, enthroned on the praises of Israel.

This volume has predominately been written with the intention to strengthen and encourage worship leaders. I strongly believe that being a worship leader is not a job - it is a calling. As worship leaders we are responsible for leading our congregations into the presence of God. It could be said that this is one of the most important callings in the world. As the text indicates above " Adonai is enthroned on the praises of His people".When we lead people in worship the heavens open and the Ruach Ha Elohim(Spirit of God) is enthroned among us. This has been for the most part a duty that has been expected to be done without specific training. Worship leaders are supposed to simply figure it out.

Most worship leaders have their fair share of cringeworthy sink or swim moments that they were told is the way that they need to learn. Granted, there is a degree of truth to this. It is often through our mistakes that we learn and we become sharpened. It is my prayer that perhaps God will use this work to sharpen you and allow you to become better worship leaders .

It is my hope that the seasoned worship leaders who read this booklet will be encouraged and refreshed by what you will read in the forthcoming pages. It is my hope that the worship leaders who are starting their journey will find themselves strengthened and that you will perhaps gain a fresh Biblical perspective and skills that took me over three decades as a worship leader to attain.

However, before we begin our study it is important that some preliminary concepts are understood.

This work is written from a Messianic Jewish Perspective. Because of this there may be certain terminology that may seem unfamiliar to you. I shall take a moment and give you a brief overview of the key words and names that will be used intermittently.

Shabbat = Sabbath
   Yeshua= Jesus
   Rav Shaul = Paul
   HaShem = God
   Adonai = Lord
   El Elyon. = Most High God
   Ruach Ha Kodesh= The Holy Spirit

All Bible passages are taken from the Tree of Life Version. The TLV is a cutting edge new translation that has been a joint venture from some of the top scholars in the Messianic Jewish Movement. The verses are used with permission .

2

Chapter 2

Why is Worship Important?

I wanted to begin our study by giving a couple of definitions for worship and Praise from a Hebraic understanding.

Shachah : To depress or prostrate in homage or loyalty to God, bow down, fall down flat

Hallal: To praise, to make a show or rave about, to glory in or boast upon, to be clamorously foolish about your adoration of God

Are these the definitions of worship and praise that you have seen active in your life?

The worship industry is a very lucrative business. Millions of dollars are made each year as believers rush to purchase the latest worship CD, DVD, Download , or attend the latest praise concert that happens to be in town each weekend. In the last 10 years the popularity of worship music has increased tenfold. It seems that the Praise and worship section at most Christian book stores has grown from two shelves to a series immense monuments filling most of the store. The same growth can be seen on digital streaming and downloading platforms. They now have a stage at every Christian music festival that is now dedicated solely to praise and worship bands. There has even been a worship evening on American Idol, in which the contestants sing worship songs and are judged on their ability to do so.

It would appear that a great deal of the popular Christian bands have made a notable effort during this time placing their usual itinerary on the shelf and releasing album after album of worship music. It seems that everyone has a worship album out nowadays, I even recently have seen a death metal worship record.

Don't get me wrong, this emphasis and apparent acceptance of praise and worship music hitting the mainstream culture seems wonderful on the surface. I have been to several acquaintance's homes in where I have seen a Hillsong Australia CD on the shelf right next to a Metallica record.I have seen a Newsboys album and a Shakira CD sitting on the seat of people's cars in the parking lot of Walmart.

This apparent cultural acceptance of praise music on the surface seems like a really good thing. It seems that now more then ever before in history people have access to righteous music and are listening to the songs contained in these worship albums and being exposed to the word of Adonai like never before.

However, there is also a major problem with this as well. To me the symbolism of this bi- cultural appearance is far too poignant to overlook. On the surface it would appear encouraging that so many people are being exposed to praise and worship music. However, if we look a little deeper we see an alarming trend- that there appears to be no difference between the sacred and the secular. Looking at the lyrics of a good deal of modern praise and worship songs it is often difficult to tell who it is that they are singing about.

I listen to a lot of praise music throughout the week in order to prepare for the Shabbat services and to look for some material to sing during the services.I have to tell you how disappointing a good portion of these lyrics tend to be. The lyrical content of a great deal of modern worship songs have become vacuous and devoid of meaning. I often cannot tell from listening to the piece, who the artist is singing about in the song, I cannot even tell for certain that they are singing about Adonai because absent from the song seem to be any specific mention of His attributes and His Holiness .A lot of these songs I cannot tell if they are singing about Yeshua or their significant other . These songs often have really shallow and vague lyrics like" I love you because of what you have done for me, you complete me in every way"

Is this lack of boldness in our praise music due to marketing reasons? Meaning that they feel that they could sell more albums if they keep the references to Yeshua purposely vague, and have a sort of **insert your name here** mentality? Or perhaps it represents an even deeper and more dire theological problem- the fact that the praise issued in the song seems estranged, distant, and unfamiliar.

Firstly, do we really know Yeshua that we worship or do merely know of Him. Secondly, have we ever been taught how to truly worship Yeshua in spirit and in truth. Let us look at a verse in John for a moment.

John 4:23-24 (TLV)

23 But an hour is coming—it is here now—when the true worshipers will worship the Father in spirit and truth, for the Father is seeking such people as His worshipers. 24 God is Spirit, and those who worship Him must worship in spirit and truth."

So as we can see, our Messiah Yeshua is giving us a little explanation of what God is looking for in our worship. He is looking for us to worship Him in Spirit and in Truth.

3

Chapter 3

Worship In Spirit

Romans 12:9-12(TLV)

9 Let love be without hypocrisy—detesting what is evil, holding fast to the good. 10 Be tenderly devoted to one another in brotherly love; outdo one another in giving honor. 11 Do not be lagging in zeal; be fervent in spirit. Keep serving the Lord, 12 rejoicing in hope, enduring in distress, persisting in prayer.

Rav Shaul (Paul) in Romans 12:11 tells us not to be "lagging in zeal." This means we are to have a passion to worship Adonai. To worship God in spirit is to praise Him with the right attitude or from the heart. In this situation the heart includes our intellect, volition, conscience and emotions. One's whole heart must be engaged in worship for it to be acceptable to God.

There is an ancient prayer that has become the pinnacle of faith for Jewish believers in Messiah Yeshua called The Shema. Within the words of this supplication lay the foundation of how we are to worship Adonai.

Deuteronomy 6:4–5 (TLV)

Shema Israel, ADONAI Eloheinu, ADONAI Echad

4 "Hear O Israel, the Lord our God, the Lord is one 5 Love Adonai your God with all your heart and with all your soul and with all your strength.

In Psalm 111:1 we see another mention of worshipping Adonai with all of your heart.

Psalm 111:1 (TLV)

1 Halleluyah! I praise Adonai with all my heart in the company and congregation of the upright.

Worship in spirit involves doing those acts which please God with the right attitude. It is possible for one to be physically present at a worship service and not be worshipping God because their attitude toward worship may not be correct. As a result, they are not worshipping God in spirit. So it is vitally important that we understand the characteristics of worship that is truly in spirit.

1. _Worship in spirit must be with understanding._
   Paul(Rav Shaul) teaches us this.

1 Corinthians 14:15 (TLV)

15 What is it then? I will pray in my spirit, but I will also pray with my mind. I will sing praises with my spirit, and I will also sing praises with my mind.

To worship with understanding(with our mind) , we must be able to comprehend what is said and done. We must appreciate the significance of each act of worship and think about what we are doing as we worship. For instance, we cannot be talking, daydreaming or sleeping during a prayer, sermon, or song and be worshipping with understanding.

2. Worship in spirit is planned and organized.
Some worship leaders prefer a "spontaneous" approach, which involves little to no planning and saying that they want to "give The RUACH (spirit) room to move which generally does not end well, and can cause awkward unprepared moments of silence.It is very important to give the Ruach Ha Kodesh (Holy Spirit) room to work in the service, however the expectation of the Ruach's interaction should never be seen as an excuse to not effectively plan the worship service. In my experience I have understood this to mean that there needs to be flexibility in the worship set for HaShem to move but lack of planning and structure often leads to confusion and often acts as a distraction to the congregation and can pull them out of their worship experience. 1 Corinthians 14:33 and 40 helps illustrate this point eloquently.

1 Corinthians 14:33 (TLV)

33 for God is not a God of confusion, but shalom. As in all the communities of the kedoshim.

1 Corinthians 14:40 (TLV)

40 But let everything be done decently and in order.

We should have an expedient order to our worship services, so that all may know what to expect and do at the appropriate times. Order is right. It is commanded of God and therefore it is good.

3. Worship in spirit is reverent or respectful to God.

We see this in Psalm 89:6-10

Psalm 89:6-10 (TLV)

6 The heavens praise Your wonders, Adonai —Your faithfulness, too—in the assembly of the kedoshim. 7 For who in the skies can compare to Adonai? Who is like Adonai among the sons of gods? 8 God is greatly feared in the council of the holy ones, and awesome above all around Him. 9 Adonai Elohei-Tzva'ot, who is like You, mighty Adonai, with Your faithfulness all around You? 10 You rule over the swelling of the sea. When its waves mount up, You still them.

Our manner of worship should reflect our respect for God and other worshippers. We are gathered to worship and praise Almighty God, therefore, we should act, speak and dress in the very best way of which we are capable. How we would dress and behave and present ourselves before a president, a royal guest, or a visiting emissary, should be simply a foretaste to how we would present ourselves before The One who Spoke the World into existence.

We should bring our best before God and show the highest degree of respect for Him.

4 Worship in spirit is sincere and springs from a holy life.

We should assemble out of love for our Heavenly Father and a desire to praise Him and commune with Him. David expresses this in Psalm 122

Psalm 122 (TLV)

I rejoiced when they said to me, "Let us go to the House of Adonai."

The time of our worship should be an occasion of great happiness and joy. We should look forward to the moment when we can assemble with our brothers and sisters in Messiah and worship Adonai . Also, our worship is not done to be seen of men, but is offered to please HaShem . Further, our worship should reflect a life of holiness. One cannot continue to live a sinful life and at the same time offer holy worship to HaShem.

Every act of worship in the assembly should be for praising and glorifying God, as well as sharpening and encouraging our fellow believers. Worship is not for self glorification or to receive the praise of people. Our efforts in worship should be to glorify God and build up our faith. Our worship to Adonai should be a blessing to one another as we assemble to get energized to stand together to face the daily onslaught of a culture that increasingly hates the righteousness of Adonai with each passing day. Like the Levites we as worship leaders are to lead the congregation into battle .

But, most importantly; worship needs to be a consistent lifestyle. As worship leaders we need to take our worship to God seriously, we need to discipline ourselves to live a life of holiness that is manifested not only when the lights of the stage and the eyes of the congregation are upon us - but also when no one is watching. In short we as worship leaders like the Levites before us have a higher calling then other believers. We have the awesome yet humbling responsibility of leading the congregation into the very presence of El Elyon. Because of this unique calling we need to be consistent with our lives. We must resist the temptation to put on an act of pretend righteousness. We must never view our job as worship leaders as a performance in which we act a role .Like the Levites before us it is expected that we live a life of purity and holiness.

4

Chapter 4

Worship In Truth

True worship that pleases God, is also to be in truth, as well as in spirit. What does it mean to worship in truth? First, we need to define "truth." The answer to that question is revealed in the prayer of Yeshua in **John 17:17.**

John 17:17 (TLV)

17 *"Make them holy in the truth. Your word is truth.*

We also see this in Psalm 119: 142

Psalm 119:142 (TLV)

142 *Your justice is righteousness forever, and Your Torah is truth.*

So when we speak of the objective truth, the truth of the Torah (Bible), we speak collectively of God's Word or His Torah. That is why I feel that it is of the utmost importance to include the reading of Scripture in the worship service. We are including

14

the ultimate truth of God's word into our worship.

By doing this we are not limited by our emotions or lack of eloquent vocabulary, we are worshipping the God of truth with the ultimate form of truth- The Torah.We are also providing a poignant transition that permeates a sacred atmosphere between worship songs.

I wanted to take a moment here, as long as we are discussing worship to address a rather divisive issue in the church, and that is worship through the arts.

5

Chapter 5

Worship and the Arts

I wanted to take a moment here to examine a verse that I am sure that we have overlooked many times. It is found in Genesis 2:19. Let us look at it together.

Genesis 2:19 (TLV)

19 Adonai Elohim had formed from the ground every animal of the field and every flying creature of the sky, so He brought them to the man to see what he would call them.

Here we see that God has given Adam the artistic freedom to name all of the animals. Adam observed all of the animals in their natural state and behavior and he gave them a name out of his own God- given artistic creativity that corresponded with those observations.Adam could have chosen not to have named all of the animals, but rather he chose to honor the talents and potential that God placed in him by using his gifts for God's intended purposes. Here we seem to see Adam sharing in the " it is good" theme that we see all through the creation account. God has delegated the task of naming all of the animals to Adam. The text states that whatever Adam named the animals was to be their names for all time. We can see here that God considered Adam's decision in the names of the animals to also be good.

God has gifted all of us with some sort of talent. For some it perhaps is excellence in musical aptitude.For others perhaps they have been blessed with a poet's pen. For some maybe they are gifted at sculpting, dancing, acting, painting, singing. Whatever our talents are, we are to use them to worship our King Yeshua. Our talents are NOT demonic, they are good in God's eyes and should be used in our expression of worship to Him.

For far too long, congregations of the Messiah have been cemeteries of the Arts. It is long past time that we start becoming a sanctuary of the Arts.

Isaiah 6 and The Three Pillars of Worship

Now that we have spent sufficient time examining why worship is vital we need to direct our attention to Isaiah 6:1-8. The text of Isaiah 6:1-8 provides for us three foundational structures or pillars that we as worship leaders can use as to arrange our worship sets and help lead our congregation into the presence of Adonai.

Isaiah 6:1-8 (TLV)

6 **In the year of King Uzziah's death, I saw** *Adonai* **sitting on a throne, high and lifted up,[a] and the train of His robe filled the Temple. 2 Seraphim were standing above Him. Each had six**

wings: with two he covered his face and with two he covered his feet, and with two he flew. 3 One called out to another, and said:"Holy, holy, holy, is *Adonai-Tzva'ot!* The whole earth is full of His glory."[b] 4 Then the posts of the door trembled at the voice of those who called, and the House was filled with smoke. [c] 5 Then I said: "*Oy* to me! For I am ruined! For I am a man of unclean lips, and I am dwelling among a people of unclean lips. For my eyes have seen the King, *Adonai-Tzva'ot!*" 6 Then one of the seraphim flew to me, with a glowing coal in his hand, which he had taken with tongs from the altar. 7 He touched my mouth with it and said: "Behold, this has touched your lips. Your iniquity is taken away, and your sins atoned for." 8 Then I heard the voice of *Adonai* saying: "Whom should I send, and who will go for Us?" So I said, "*Hineni.* Send me."

I am convinced that worship needs to be transformational. It is not enough to merely sing a couple of choruses as a ritualistic nicety and segway to the sermon. Rather, worship needs to be life changing and leave a lasting impact that only occurs by being in the presence of God. The most profound evidence of this is found in Isaiah 6:1-8. In this text we see three specific pillars that eloquently demonstrate what should occur during our worship experience.

I Know Who You Are Worshipping (Personal Relationship With Yeshua).

This seems rather obvious, but yet the importance of this reality cannot be over emphasized. In order to worship Yeshua we must have a clear vision of who He is. We must see the Lord exalted, sitting on the throne of the universe in all His majestic glory. If we do not know that Yeshua is the Messiah , how can we truly worship him. If we have yet to ask Him into our hearts , and experience the freedom from our sins and receive the empowerment of the Ruach Ha Kodesh in our lives, how can we truly worship Him?

This would be like going down the street and walking into the first random stranger's house that we see, to hug everyone affectionately and to sit down at the dinner table with the family and to begin to converse with the family living there about your day. This seems ridiculous. But it brings full circle my point earlier in our discussion , if you do not have the Ruach ha Kodesh (The Holy Spirit) in your life, if you have yet to be forgiven for your sins that have separated you from God- it is not possible for you to truly worship God. If you are not redeemed, how can you sing the songs of the redeemed? All that the worship music will be to you,will be a collection of nice melodies, uplifting words and miscellaneous niceties that you will not be able to connect to with any depth. There most likely will be NO life change, and to you it will be just another set of nice songs to put on your CD rack or your digital library next to your Lady Gaga album.

Romans 10:9-10 (TLV)

9 For if you confess with your mouth that *Yeshua* is Lord, and believe in your heart that God raised Him from the dead, you will be saved. 10 For with the heart it is believed for righteousness, and with the mouth it is confessed for salvation.

II Conviction of Sin

A deep sense of humility is imperative in our worship. A deep conviction of unworthiness is the natural reaction that we have when we are in the presence of God. As we can see from our Isaiah 6 model, when Isaiah encountered the glory of God

A. *Conviction Isaiah verses 6:1-5 (TLV)*

God is perfect and Holy in all His actions. When we encounter the manifest presence of God we who are infirm are brought face to face with our own iniquities and shortcomings.

In this pillar the Holy Spirit reveals our sins to us. We are made aware of **(convicted)** what we need to change and where we have personally fallen short of God's glorious standard. In a worship set these are usually songs that edify the nature of God and focus on His ultimate holiness and our ultimate lack of ability to live a holy life on our own accord. This pillar reminds us of our need for him, and the redemptive atoning work of His precious son Yeshua.

B. *Cleansing Isaiah verses 6:6- 7 (TLV)*

In First John 1:9 it eloquently states the following;

1 John 1:9 (TLV)

9 If we confess our sins, He is faithful and righteous to forgive our sins and purify us from all unrighteousness.

That is a promise from God that states a twofold truth. Firstly, it shows that repentance is a needed and frequent element of our faith. Secondly, it promises that when we honestly confess our sins the Lord will forgive us. Just as Isaiah was **cleansed** by the coal to his lips, we are **cleansed** by the precious blood that Yeshua shed for us on the execution stake. In this pillar we are lead to ask the Lord for forgiveness for our sinful and selfish actions. In a worship set these songs are characterized by displaying a theme of repentance and are usually slower and heartfelt. This pillar is designed to take us from merely being made aware of our sinfulness to throwing ourselves at the mercy of a loving God who is waiting to forgive us. We need to take the initiative to approach the throne of grace boldly. This pillar allows us to do that.

III Surrender Isaiah verse 6: 8–13 (TLV)

The final pillar in the Isaiah 6 model is Surrender. According to the text it was only after proceeding through the steps of Conviction and Cleansing that Isaiah was able to respond to the call of God on his life. Likewise it is only though ridding ourselves of the remnants of our sins that we can truly hear the still- small voice of the Holy Spirit directing our paths. This pillar allows us to de-clutter our spiritual lives so that the light of God's glory can shine gloriously through the window of our souls unabated, and when this occurs it allows us to share His marvelous light with a world hopelessly plagued by darkness.

Isaiah audibly heard God's call upon his life as soon as he had been cleansed from the stains of his sins.Before we can serve the Lord we must first surrender to Him and to the call and commission that He has for us. We are not called to be successful, but we are expected to be available.

So to reiterate, I have learned to view worship as having three pillars or layers.

We need to personally know God in order to worship Him. As we experience God in His holiness we are convicted of our sins and ungodliness and we cry out to God for mercy.

We repent of our sins and are cleansed from our unrighteousness. It is this stage that we are cleansed and we are able to hear from God.

We surrender to His will for our lives and respond to the direction that we are called to go in.

The bottom line here is that in the end, it is OUR responsibility to seek out God and to enter into worship. We must never let our own personal musical tastes alone determine whether a worship service is anointed or not.

In closing it needs to be mentioned that all of these steps are equally as important. All three balance off each other, and are interdependent. The removal of one pillar causes the destruction and desolation of what is being supported. Used in unison they provide an impenetrable foundation for the truth resting on them. It is my strong opinion that following this biblical model of worship is the most effective way to (directed by the Ruach Ha Kodesh) shatter the mediocrity and stagnancy that so often plagues our modern churches, and to lead your congregation in life changing worship.

www.ingramcontent.com/pod-product-compliance
Lightning Source LLC
Chambersburg PA
CBHW050753180726
48003CB00020B/2548